Heavenly Highway Hymns

Gospel Stylings for Solo Piano
by Roger Bennett

Moderately Advanced

Lillenas PUBLISHING COMPANY

KANSAS CITY, MO 64141

CONTENTS

Joy Unspeakable

BARNEY E. WARREN
Arr. by Roger Bennett

5

Send the Light

CHARLES H. GABRIEL
Arr. by Roger Bennett

Wayfaring Stranger

Traditional Spiritual
Arr. by Roger Bennett

Plaintively, with a shuffle ♩ = ca. 88

The Gloryland Way

J. S. TORBETT
Arr. by Roger Bennett

Moving along ♩ = ca. 112

detached

It Is Well with My Soul

PHILIP P. BLISS
Arr. by Roger Bennett

Thoughtfully ♩ = ca. 88

He Keeps Me Singing

LUTHER B. BRIDGERS
Arr. by Roger Bennett

Land Where Living Waters Flow

MOSIE LISTER
Arr. by Roger Bennett

Wait 'Til You See Me in My New Home

JOE PARKS
Arr. by Roger Bennett

Relaxed ♩ = ca. 92

Faster, with a shuffle ♩ = ca. 112

36

Fast ragtime feel ♩ = ca. 84

Down on My Knees

MOSIE LISTER
Arr. by Roger Bennett

Moderately ♩ = ca. 112

Where We'll Never Grow Old

JAMES C. MOORE
Arr. by Roger Bennett